STIGMAS
TO HINDRANCES

STIGMAS
TO HINDRANCES

India: Fight Back

MANPREET OLA

Notion Press

Old No. 38, New No. 6
McNichols Road, Chetpet
Chennai - 600 031

First Published by Notion Press 2017
Copyright © Manpreet Ola 2017
All Rights Reserved.

ISBN 978-1-946869-00-5

To my sister,

Hardika ola,

Who always encouraged me to follow my
dreams and trusted me when i doubted myself.

CONTENTS

ACKNOWLEDGEMENTS

This is my first book and I am very grateful to my parents Karan Singh Ola and Sumitra Ola for encouraging me to work on something which I never thought I would be able to; throughout my journey during this book writing, they were very supporting, patient and a strong guiding force. I completely dedicate this book to my sister Hardika Ola, who always had faith in me, trusted me and would always look after me so that I never lose faith in myself. The role that my brother Mandeep played in my development as an independent, self sufficient and hardworking person cannot go unacknowledged. I would like to thank my friend Ankita, who has been a constant supporter of my dream to be an author.

I am grateful to the entire Notion press team, firstly for accepting to work with me on my book and secondly to guide me step by step patiently since the beginning.

This book would not take shape without the various storytellers of our country, who wrote beautiful pieces of art so that one is encouraged to express themselves through writing.

Every morning I wake up
With a dream in my eye
To capture my aims
And to write my name in sky
Every morning I wake up
My dream takes me a little deeper
Like a dose of honey in the bee hive
The far away candle looks closer with every
passing morning
And the every upcoming dream
Soars my hopes a little higher
Every morning after I wake up
I am left with nothing but with wonderment
Will I ever be there?
Will I ever conquer, what I aspire for
Will my name ever be written in sky?
Will my day ever get bright?
Or will my dreams just get crumpled, like
every following dark night.

Every morning after I wake up

I wonder like those of my fellow sisters

Who sit in the midst of the sands and oils?

Hoping one day, our minds will be allowed to
wither

With the blowing wind

Hoping one day, the sky will roar and set us
free from the open captivity

Where ironically, in our own houses

We are nothing but fellow prisoners

Who dared, to take birth

Who dared, to survive

Who with heavy hearts just trampled our
own desires?

Every morning after I wake up

I am left with nothing but despair

Because the world so huge

Took our shine like that of the moon by
the clouded sky

Every morning after I wake up

I just wish, I can dream some more.

❧

1. Rights of a Woman

India, such a vast country with various beautiful traditions, rituals, customs but despite of all the beauty there is one thing which always makes me curious that when since birth onwards we are taught to respect our elders, pay our regards to them, touch their feet and seek their blessings, we were always taught that our parents are a reflection of God. In earlier days students, were sent to school just to learn basic manners, there they were taught the importance of their parents, how if they misbehave with them or don't respect them then God punishes them, yet despite of being ingrained with hard core values and purpose as we turn into adults we are deprived of this basic duty of ourselves. We the females of our country aren't allowed to love our parents as we loved them when we were kids, we aren't allowed to show a little gratitude monetarily, why we are treated differently than our fellow male siblings who were raised like we were, who went to the schools with similar values, why are the females not given equal rights as their male counterparts, not that I want rights such as going out at night, which again we shouldn't be deprived of, but presently the viewpoint is about being treated equally with respect to taking care of our parents like our brothers do it, why can't the earning adult female be allowed to take care of the household expenses. All of us very willingly would want to act responsibly. Not that we aren't aware of the fact that according to our societal values after the girl is married off, she has to accept her husband's home as her home; but it doesn't mean that after marriage our dynamics with our parents change or the love that we have for them reduces to a lesser level, yet the society imposes such harsh restrictions on our lifestyles that if the girl pays the household expenses then the father returns the child's cash through numerous ways such as gifting her gold, or gifting their son in law something expensive, sometimes this forces us to wonder whether this ritual of dowry must have been maintained by the parents of the girl child only; who live under this impression that if they don't pay the in laws with gifts and cash then the in laws will misbehave and trouble their daughter.

And I think even they can't be blamed this has become the norm of our society where the first question our relatives ask the father is "how much ransom did you pay." But this isn't my point the only thing which makes one curious is why does the society make the parents of a girl child feel embarrassed when she is running the house, why in this fast growing economy where girls are standing equal to boys in numerous sectors and in some far better than them, aren't allowed to take care of their expenses, why does a father have to lower his head when the girl child isn't married, on the other hand if the male child isn't married, no one has any inputs or suggestions to make.

When a female decides to stay with their parents and take care of them, then the society starts doubting a girls character or the father is judged to be in capable of getting his daughter married, the society starts doubting the source of income of the girl child, she is cross checked for her caliber, eyes are wide opened if she is seen to be smarter than her male siblings, this innocent family becomes the talk of the town, just because she dared to take a step towards creating a society which treats all its members equally, the right with which our constitution has given us the whole leverage of.

All the females of this country are pretty much clear with their duties and responsibilities towards their married life and in no way, they aim to run away from that, but our society needs to be receptive enough to understand that our girls are capable enough for multi tasking, they are pretty much clear what is expected of them in our culture, what roles they have to fulfill, but just adding another role of taking care of their own parents won't make them any less capable. It is high time we start developing faith on our girls and set them free to play this role also as beautifully as they play the others, otherwise it is no point for us to run to make our mark globally because soon the world will realize the hollowness, which lies within our society.

2. Caste and Its Troubles

Casteism is not something which is new for Indians; we are clearly familiar with the role played by caste system in social stratification where the Hindus are divided into four main castes based on their duties and work, i.e. the Brahmins which are the priests and the teachers; Kshatriyas who were the warriors and the rulers; the Vaishyas, whose prime task was farming or trading and lastly are the Shudras who were seen as the laborers or those who were assigned menial tasks. These four main castes are further stratified into various thousands of castes and sub castes which dictates the kind of job they will take up. Initially in ancient times this caste system divided our society into various upper and lower castes, where the individuals falling under the upper caste were bestowed with privileges and respect; while those falling under the category of lower castes were treated with disrespect and were considered as untouchables, which made the life of these individual very depressing, they would always be mistreated by the upper caste people, they would be given left over's to eat, even if they were working as servants, they weren't allowed to enter the kitchens and cook; they weren't allowed to sit equal or next to their masters, there were numerous incidents where it was reported that dalit children who were enrolled in schools due to the pressures from the government weren't allowed to attend classes instead they would be asked to broom the campus or the classroom, and when other children observed such behavior towards them , they started bullying them, harassing them, misbehaving with them etc. To uplift the people of lower castes from all this after independence, government started with quota system, where various educational organizations and occupational sectors would provide few seats to these under privileged individuals, who were as human as the upper caste individuals, but were facing the brunt of deprivation due to our rigid hierarchy system; also the constitution banned discrimination on the basis of caste system, which was a very strong and a positive step towards removing the disadvantages and injustices that these people were facing over the years. The reservation in jobs which was started in 1950's which was initially for the scheduled castes and the scheduled tribe was extended to the other backward classes in the 1980's. But over the years, due to rapid technological advancement, urbanizations, increased literacy rates individuals have become more sensitive to such grave issues and to a great extent have become accommodating of the inter differences which are prevalent in the various castes, also people have learnt to live cooperatively with each other due to which the various lower castes which were deprived of various opportunities initially are to an extent not facing the same difficulties which they were facing in earlier times and they are being provided equal resources, they are given equal leverages, they are provided with equal opportunities; despite of all these changes every now and then we see that some or the other caste raises an issue for reservation in the occupational and educational sector. The point is not to provide various individuals with less options, but the question is despite of everyone getting equal, why are some people still given the leverage of performing less than other individuals, why is the competition not equal for everybody, why isn't there equal representation for different individuals coming from different castes applying for the same posts, why are some individuals given an easy access to the same position for which both the equally deserving individuals are struggling. To an extent even this is acceptable that there actually are individuals in our country who are still struggling in the rural areas who do not have sufficient resources to eat a daily course meal, they can't afford school for their children, there are still people who aren't earning enough to get well acquainted with technology for whom owning a Nokia handset is still a big thing, and radio is actually the only source of entertainment. And for such individuals I am sure all of us are ready to compromise so that even these fellow brothers and sisters of ours can study, eat well, earn a livelihood where they can provide the basic necessities of life which even their families deserve as much as ours, such individuals truly deserve reservation in the educational and occupational sectors so that they aren't left far behind from other fellow citizens.

Now coming to the point where all of us feel disappointed is when those individuals who aren't economically deprived, who can afford luxurious cars, those who can carry expensive gadgets, who are enrolled in good schools by their families, instead of being present in the classes and studying something; they come out on the streets and protest for reservations, this unfairness in our system is problematic, when such individuals are provided with opportunities by investing less resources be it in the form of hard work or money, this creates differences of opinion and all these issues are forcing us all to pursue for options outside India and not because we aren't capable of showing our talents here, but because the hard working individuals are not given equal opportunities to prove our worth, when time comes to stand our grounds the quota system creates barriers and those not falling under reservations are left far behind. It is saddening to see the hard core reality of our country that all those individuals who come from similar backgrounds and similar experiences have to face different results, where the General category people have to work to get 95 percent the OBC's can achieve the same post by just getting an 80 percent, the question is does the government think the General category people are given some extra medicine to increase their brain power that they will be able to work hard and achieve that position easily, if the faith in the General category is so high then don't let failure be a taboo, don't let people define one's capabilities on the basis of marks, or the number of degrees a person holds, or the government post a person is posted on, because this reservation system of our country is creating differences in two friends coming from different backgrounds, it is creating breeding grounds for hatred, it is becoming nothing but a field for battle, the vote bank policy of our country is creating disasters within ourselves, all these differences makes individuals insecure, it makes them doubt their potentials which is hampering the mental well being of our citizens.

3. Religious Offerings

In our country religion, holds great importance; it isn't just a mere concept but our entire Indian system is based and revolves around the various religions, there are various religions in our country, majority of citizens follow the Hinduism, then the Islam which is followed by Muslims, after this comes Christians who follow Christianity, then there are people following Jainism, Buddhism and others. Though all the religions and the various beliefs that we hold with them have taught us very positive things, with the help of various religious beliefs there is strong unity amongst the citizens, these strong beliefs create a sense of fraternity, in a very positive light they set an example of India all over the world of the various rich value system and principles. If we ask ourselves regarding the importance of our religion in our lives, we can go on and on making praises in its name. Despite of all these good things about our religion, it is very crucial that we understand the hatred it's creating amongst us, how this whole concept whose whole purpose is to unite us, to see a common thing amongst each other and to respect the differences which people coming from the various religions hold. How we have ignored the whole fact that our religion is our identity to an extent, but it doesn't make any individual belonging to the other religion inferior to us, in no way if your neighbor is a Hindu or a Muslim makes him any less of a human being. All the individuals who take birth in this world are comprised of basic sentiments and emotions, all of us are innocent beings born with emotions free of hatred, we weren't sent on earth with the motive of proving one religion superior to others, nor were we born with the religious tag of being a Hindu, or a Christian.

Shockingly in our country the fight is not only about showing superiority of one religion over the other but the various superstitious customs which are prevailing fully fledged, where self proclaimed Guru's have opened their Ashram's and have started some sort of business with their followers under the influence of which illiterate individuals belonging to rural background who are facing difficulties and problems in their lives are provided with easy remedies to get rid of their troubles by making sacrifices in the name of Almighty. Initially these sacrifices comprised of keeping fasts, feeding beggars, etc. etc, which in reality were really beneficial for the individual not literally the person got rid of his difficulties, but indirectly benefited the beggar and keeping fasts to an extent was considered healthy for the body also. But the problem which started increasing gradually was the level of sacrifices an individual had to make in the name of God, sometimes he would be asked to offer his cattle in the name of God in some full moon night which would help him get rid of his troubles, but till now if we think logically we can't make sense of how offering a buffalo to God can help someone get rid of diseases, or make one prosperous, or help get someone's daughter get married or in some cases make someone pregnant. Not that I am an atheist or nor in any way I am against our customs and traditions, but in each and every way I am against all those self proclaimed saints who are taking advantage of innocence of others, or using their trust negatively and asking innocent human beings to kill their children, sacrifice their own lives in the name of God and are putting rubbish in their heads that abiding by these senseless customs will bring prosperity in their lives. It is really important that we understand it's not the sole responsibility of these impersonators but all those followers, the neighbors, the society who know the repercussions of such heinous acts in the lives of the victim but still introduce innocent families, take advantage of their plights and expose them to such harsh situations where they feel the only escape from their troubles is killing their children, or leaving them for a night with these baba's, who take advantage of their circumstances and force themselves on these innocent beings. Every now and then our news channels are showing some or the other incident where on the advice of fake baba's children get killed, young girls get raped, animals are slaughtered.

It is essential for the upliftment of our society that we take strong measures against this, we need to ask questions from ourselves, that does after making all these sacrifices, do these people get what they had wished for? Are they able to sleep in peace? Don't the screams of their children or their pet animals haunt them? And if the answers to these questions in no way satisfy you, it is time we learn to act against such elements and stop being a part of such illogical practices and save other fellow countrymen of ours from losing their lives due to these practices.

4. Justice Delayed Is Justice Denied

Before starting with another crucial factor about our country which needs to be worked upon, it is essential we ask ourselves one very basic question, whether how seriously do we take our constitution? How essential it is for us to stick to our preamble? And if at all to prove ourselves very patriotic we answer, pretty seriously, then I think it is time we go back to revise what it states. Our preamble which comprises of various rights that we deserve, one of them being "justice" in itself, the very crucial word has lost its importance, if we go back to our courts and open case logs and records, we can clearly see there are numerous cases which have been filed long back and till now those cases have not even been discussed, leave apart providing justice to the victims. If we conduct a survey, through this only we will get our answer that it has been decades for numerous cases where people are waiting for the first hearing of the cases, they aren't getting appointments, few people do not even get lawyers to represent their case, and by luck if someone gets a lawyer to fight the case, then their fees is far beyond what a poor individual can pay. Our constitution very sincerely has mentioned about "justice, social, economic and political" which clearly means that the citizen of India will be treated with fair means in the social, economic and political arenas, and in reality, this basic essential right of ours is snatched from us, any court starting from district court to the others, where there are so many cases which are lying pending, cupboards are stacked with files, dust settling on them, cobwebs have formed on them, but the poor victim hasn't got rid of the problem, for which he is desperately looking for a solution; it seems that our legal system is trying to protect the spiders from becoming homeless.

Surprisingly if any case hearing has started, then the harmful elements of our society start working against the innocent individuals who filed the cases to expect honesty and justice, and all this is clearly prevalent in cases where the opponent is a strong influential individual. It is essential to understand the rationale of honesty taking a different stance in case of powerful opponents. Our legal system at times have become a money making business where no one is concerned about what is ethically and morally right, in fact the money in the individuals pocket will decide the course of the outcome. There are so many cases that are heard in the courtrooms daily, to state a few, dowry cases, cases for child's custody, domestic violence, work place violence, sexual assaults, physical abuses, rape, kidnapping, murders and property feuds. In all these surprisingly women are more likely to be the victims, if the opposition is a male member and he has strong political connections, or is rich and can pay bribe for the outcome to be in their favor, then the poor girl is doomed, because then our legal system actually starts acting as if they are blindfolded, then they aren't concerned about the self respect of the women, then the dignity of women is at stake, because to prove their point, the opposition will go to any extent, if that means, getting an eye witness killed, or verbally insulting the women by asking inappropriate questions, raising issues regarding her character, not only this if at all a girl is ready to bear all this humiliation in the court room, then she is very likely to get threatening calls blackmailing her regarding the safety and well being of her family members and her own life; and surprisingly this isn't a plot of any movie, but a hard core reality of our legal system where a women has to think twice before accepting things to turn out in her favor, if at all it involves a high profile case then the person can think of thanking her stars that all the stardom and publicity might turn the chairs towards her, but if a woman belonging to middle or a lower socio economic strata expects justice then she has to be prepared to lose face in front of the society, cause justice for her doesn't come easily, arranged on a platter. It is really essential that there needs to be some changes that need to be made, in our perspectives or our thinking so that going to fight for justice doesn't become taboo for girls and women, who have as much right to expect justice as their male counterparts; it is crucial that we understand that a case filed for divorce by a woman shouldn't be an eye opener for the society, this woman has all the rights to walk out of a marriage which is harming her mental and physical well being, she shouldn't be ridiculed or face humiliation in the court room; she should feel comfortable to fight bravely and as calmly as the male counterpart; why should her demand for justice raise questions for her family and her character; why should a woman's family face humiliation and torture when their daughter decided to avail her rights; it is essential for us to answer how does one's pocket size determine the outcome of the case. It is essential we suggest making stringent laws against those committing heinous acts, so that our legal system is burdened less with such cases and the perpetuators think twice before indulging into such acts, due to the potency of the punishment size.

5. Horrors of Rape

Every morning with the rising of the sun, a new day starts, which brings with it many new opportunities, new hopes, new beginnings which work to cover up the lost time, the passed away day, things we couldn't accomplish so far, another chance to fight our battles, but as soon as we get hold of the newspaper, or our cell phones, or switch on the televisions sets, we get surrounded by ample news and amongst them which creates the greatest havoc is the news regarding rapes, sexual and physical abuses, kidnapping, murders, acid attacks in one sided love. These headlines which ruin our day in today's time's have become a sort of routine, if any day we wake up and we aren't told such things it feels so incomplete, every day when we feel our daughters are safe, there comes some or the other fuming headline regarding molestation.

We have had governments coming and going one after the other, all made promises regarding subsidies in gas cylinders, corruption free India, terrorism free India, black money ridden India, discounts in grains, surprisingly all of them promised crime free country but nor did once they mentioned about safe India for our women, the crimes that they focused on were the crimes done by the opposition such as black mailing, hoarding cash, exploiting the poor for votes through cash and liquor, but no one promised or assured us for the safety of our girls, if at all these resolutions were taken up, they weren't ever implemented as fully fledged as the demonetization or as the protests for reservation by various castes in occupational opportunities. No one took to it seriously to make stringent laws against those who groped girls in bars, in public gatherings, against those culprits who would not want to miss a chance of touching a woman inappropriately in any place, at any time of the day. There were very loud voices which always rose and will continue to rise when they will see girls wearing skirts, shorts, jeans, or if girls are seen entering bars, cafes, if they are seen with male friends. The society always through some or the other reason finds a way to blame the victim for every incident she faces, if it's an acid attack, due to one sided love, people will argue it was because the girl must have given some hints, she must have walked in some typical pattern, which must have given hints, or must have fought with the male, which might have hurt his ego.

Since a decade these things have increased to such a level that now our parents fear when we tell them we want to move out of a city and go to a new place to look for jobs, or pursue higher studies, that they would prefer we become home makers then become independent because the society has become unsafe, where atleast even if you don't earn a living, atleast you aren't raped, assaulted, ridiculed or humiliated without any fault of yours.

There have been so many schemes by the government so that female foeticide can be completely eradicated and without any doubt all these schemes are worth applauding but the thing which further forces us to ponder over is, when the government so strongly wants the girls to survive, then why aren't they taking and adopting stricter measures to protect the same girl child when she grows up, is it another form of hypocrisy, or does our society really care about our women; and if it cares then why every now and then there are activists giving speeches regarding the dressing sense of our girl's, why is the society busy justifying these horrendous acts through explanation being imposed on the timing of the incident, place of the incident, dressing of the victim, the company the victim was hanging out with, her lifestyle; why does these things become excuses to let the culprit run away from the consequences of his acts, why aren't there stricter measures like castration, why doesn't this option seem feasible, why, is it because the families fear their sons will experience pain? And if yes, then what is the rationale for the pain faced by all those victims who were penetrated with iron rods, glass bottles or plastic or oil bottles, etc.

Why aren't we sensitive enough regarding the emotions of those who are stabbed without any fault of theirs, why are people defending such acts by giving a justification stating the modern women has become too out spoken and she needs to be taught a lesson, she has been exposed to wrong things while studying hence she needs to stay behind the four walls of her house otherwise she will start blabbering, or in some cases our society is ready with justifications such as a women's place is inside the house and if she will go out then obviously she is likely to get raped, why?

These excuses are so disgusting, when on one end, we want to excel in everything and contrasting on the other we want to suppress the voices, the freedom, and the opportunities of our women. We want to set an example for the whole world, that our country is incredible, we promote so much of tourism, we celebrate every occasion and festivals with pomp and glory, but in the midst of all these things we have some or the other incident reported stating mishappening against girls and very disturbingly, it's not that there is a bar on the age group who become victims of all these incidents, the perpetrator can make anyone the victim, a new born baby is as likely to get raped as an 80 year old woman. It's time we understand that this infant was not dressed inappropriately, she wasn't giving any signals to a male friend, she wasn't out with her friends drinking alcohol, nor was this old woman attending any late night parties, or giving any hints.

A few months back in a job interview, the interviewer asked "why is there so much violence around us" and I answered "cause sir, violence sells;" then months passed, long gone the interview and here I am, pondering about the interview and the same question.

But instead of the answer that I gave, I analyzed a very important point and realized that no it's not that the "violence sells", it's basically "our weaknesses rule" and that is why there is so much violence around us.

Finally I got my answer and then I looked deeper and realized if it's a weakness, then how can it rule? Isn't it supposed to just bend and give way to the strengths, but no, how can that happen; it was predicted long ago by our ancestors, that soon the time will come, where the devils will rule the world, the liars will succeed and the honest will be killed, belittled and shockingly; see all that is coming true.

What is the weakness that holds us down, and is not holding the criminals to the ground? If we look within us, then we can answer this, that it's none other than our one and only killer "our fear ." It is this fear within us which is making us depend on the government to protect our daughters, when we can come together to celebrate our festivals, when we can raise our voices and demand for reservations, when we can cheer up and raise the confidence of our players and when we can go on rallies and elect one political party over the other, then can't we all stand united and take steps to curb this issue of our society which is causing us sleeplessness, which is becoming our weakness, which is reducing our level of tourism, due to which, tourists are avoiding visiting our country out of the fear to their safety. Can't we all let this hindrance be curbed to make India a safer country to live for our females, because it's important we remember that it is the same country which worships a female "Goddess Laxmi" for wealth; "Goddess Durga" for power and lastly "Goddess Saraswati" for education. All our religions which are a strong part of our identity have always taught us the value of a female in our society and if we can't learn to be true and honest to our religious values then it doesn't make sense of fighting on its name for your rights, because our rights comprise also of the right to live with dignity and if our females continue to be victims then we are depriving them of this right.

It is for us to realize that a problem is not solved just by discussing it, or by placing the blame on others, nor with the help of giving futile judgments, but just by taking steps to act on it, by coming together to fight it, it is time we realize that the innocent dreams are being destroyed and broken by inhumanity and it is only with the combined support and help that we can overcome it.

"Act now my ladies, so that the fire within you, doesn't get wasted, but burns along with it the fury of your fears and the hands of those, who reach to harm you; act now so that your dignity and self respect doesn't go for a toss ."

6. OCCUPATIONAL CALIBER

I will start my new chapter with a short story. I hail from a middle class family, from a small town in India, where since we were born, we always read about in newspapers regarding people becoming inspectors, engineers or doctors, hence even my grandparents had decided the profession for me and my siblings, where the eldest was to study and become a doctor, the middle child was provided material and guidance to become an engineer, while for me, I was left with the option to choose to become an inspector; amazingly my elder sister grew up to be a doctor as was expected of her, my brother turned out to be an engineer and last it was my turn to be an inspector, I worked very hard, equal to my siblings, but no I didn't turn out to be an inspector. Without a doubt I was always impressed by police inspectors or army officers, I always felt I would be one of them someday, but I think destiny didn't have that option for me, but nor do I regret it, nor do I blame my destiny for the same; because I think it is really nice that I didn't fall in the trap of giving importance to only these three professions. This isn't just the story of my life, but this is the hard fact of our country where as soon as a child is born, the society starts making guesses for his or her future, they are taken to get their astrological predictions made, where their careers are decided. But I really want to know, if an individual doesn't fall in these three occupations, does it signify anything about his intelligence level. Not that in any way my family judged me after I didn't fall in the pre decided regime, nor did they judge my caliber, instead they trusted me with my potential, for which I will always be grateful. But it is very important for us to understand, not that those who become doctors, engineers or inspectors are in any way following some stereotypical patterns and conforming to the society, but it is completely their wish to become one of these, simultaneously for those who are taking up various other career options such as professors, artists, musicians, actors, politicians, laborers, academicians, journalists, home makers, mental health professionals, writers and many more are not in any way any less talented. We all have become so educated, India's literacy rate is rising rapidly which is completely due to increased awareness and various affordable government policies, which are commendable. It is essential that we come out of our shells and start becoming more acceptable of everyone around us, more appreciative of what others are doing professionally, it is very crucial that we understand the importance of each and every human being present regardless of what his occupation is, why despite of being one of the well educated country our tolerance levels are less for those who aren't at a better occupational level than you, why are the sweepers treated with less respect, why after becoming rich famous workers, when we go to the restaurants, we treat the waiters with disrespect, why don't we behave and follow basic etiquettes when we interact with laborers, why does an individual's profession decide the amount of respect he or she deserves. When the newer generations share their career goals with their parents and they wish to become artists, why does people put them in a stereotypical bracket, where they are labeled as useless, who won't make enough money, how does one's choice of occupation decide his value in our country. Why do we make assumptions that if someone has decided to become home maker, that person must not have been well versed in studies? It is important for us to understand that one's grades don't decide a person's choice of occupation, an equally bright child might prefer to be sitting idle and an equally dull child might aspire to become a businessman.

In our society people are judged and compared to their neighbors on the degrees the child possesses. If we go to look for a bride or a groom we ask for the educational qualification, I am not saying that it is wrong, but I am surely saying that is not the right way to determine the nature of the person. Does the person who earns his living by driving cars not working hard enough to provide for all the luxuries he can for his family, I understand that when we look for suitable mate for our children we look for those who match our socio economic strata, but it is essential that we understand there are numerous professions, now days there are vast career options available for individuals, we need to become more accepting of the various individual differences and not label and judge a person on the basis of his occupational choice, a musician is as worthy to make his name as is the doctor, there is no profession which is bigger than the other. If we wake up in the morning and the maid doesn't show up, judging on the basis of dependence level we can clearly figure out how irritable we will get, then as the day passes in the office the data operator doesn't report to work, then sending all the mails across becomes another headache, as we proceed in the day and to get rid of all this irritability and to change our state of mind we switch on the radio, and there is sudden announcement that artists and musicians will not be performing for us anymore, then the level of monotony crosses all boundaries, surely we will have our doctors to put a pill down our throat, but there will be no enjoyment, no luxury, no relaxation without these important people, whom we have learnt to take it for granted and shower with nothing but disrespect, we aren't anyone to judge someone's character on the basis of her choice of occupation, even if it is a sex worker, we call them by various names, always disrespect them, think less of them but it is high time we need to open our minds, that what a person does in his profession is completely his or her choice, whatever a person is doing atleast they are making a living for themselves, they aren't standing in front of us to earn money without any work. We aren't the right person to determine a person's intellectual skills on the basis of his work, if someone is a servant that doesn't mean they work any less than the other big shot professions; their task is equally tiring and exhausting as is ours. Also they know their task better than you know their job, and only they themselves can perform it so well, we might display skills to cook for a day or two, but still we won't be cooking as well as the chef does it, nor will we be able to fill our drinks so well as the bartender is serving it; hence it is time we give the due respect to all the professions and not make assumptions regarding people on the basis of their occupational skills, because let's face it, no one can entertain us as well as the actors, no one can treat us as well as the doctors and the mental health professionals, our house would be a mess if it wouldn't be for our maids and servants, we would not get acquainted with the world if it wouldn't be for our reporters and journalists, crime wouldn't be controlled if it wouldn't be for the brave inspectors and officers of army, navy and air force, we wouldn't be able to connect with the rest of the world if it wouldn't be for our engineers, who have made us technologically advanced, we couldn't appreciate the beauty and style of the world if we wouldn't have our artists, beauticians, designers and architects, we wouldn't be surviving if our farmers didn't grow for us and they wouldn't survive if their home makers wouldn't have supported them and very importantly things wouldn't be managed in a country if we didn't have our politicians, and lastly we wouldn't become what we have become, if we didn't have our teachers; therefore it is time we respect individuals for who they are, then for the degrees they possess.

7. Bribe the Corrupt

Before we continue any further, it is essential to ask ourselves one very crucial thing, have we all lost all our moral and ethical values, everywhere we look, we see the value of money, all our news channels are always showering us with important headlines surrounding the amount of bribe one paid to get a particular task done, while travelling in metro's or other public transport we can hear people talk to their colleagues about how their other colleague got a particular advantage by buying gifts for their bosses, how there are sting operations showing government officers being bribed or the private sector employees organizing luncheons for senior officers to get the luxuries of an office life. Shockingly it's not just the case with offices in various sectors, but it's more like the trend or a ritual that we follow starting from fellow peons to those holding privileged chairs, if we want a plumber to attend to our complains early then we have to bribe him, if we want our maids to stay loyal and honest to us than we have to bribe them, which is such an irony that first make someone corrupt and then expect for loyalty, to even get menial jobs done

The point isn't that it is wrong to gift our colleagues or our bosses if the whole motive behind is a positive thanking gesture or a season's greeting, but the fault is when this gifting becomes the criteria on the basis of which one's true caliber gets hidden, if we encourage this practice, then all those individuals who truly deserve an opportunity lose it just because this idea didn't hit him hard that get your way by "licking upwards and kicking downwards ."

Now the main question that arises is, what is up with all this bribing, why is it working full fledged in every sector of our society, why does a person's pocket size determine the sort of treatment he will receive, or the promotion he will receive, if everything has to be based on this, then why are we all studying, let's catch hold of powerful and influential people and get our chores done, indulge into crimes at increasing speed and come out innocent from the legal sentence, why dream that our children's hard work and efforts will pay, let's just look for rich people and get settled so that we have sufficient cash to buy presents to please others.

It is important for us all to come together to analyze the issue, is it that the per capita income in our country is very low and the basis expenses very high that we have to look for other sources of income, through ransoms and bribes; because shockingly it's our whole country which is under the influence of this evil habit, whether it is the administrative sector, the legal system, the education sector, the film industry, the government offices, the private sector, the health care sector, etc.

If we have cash, then we have all the cards in our favor. If the root cause behind the bribe is the low wages then it is time the government makes amendments and increases the pay scales, so that we do not have to stoop so low, that we start doubting our potentials and learn to take the easy road of buttering up powerful people to reach a higher position, because if this continues then the whole cycle will never break and when we become leaders we will expect our juniors to abide by the same custom and if they fail to do so, it will shatter our egos and will fail the real caliber of our junior.

After paying attention to this obstruction clearly, we can realize, it's not only the low wages that are the source for breeding this corruption, but the greed for money, we have taken it very seriously that we should always strive for more and never feel satisfied and whole heartedly we are applying it to this sin.

8. Generation Gap

As time passes, the generations and their trends also change, with each passing generation there are numerous things which becomes trends and as with evolving time new generations come up they bring along with themselves some other advancements and fashion. But the latest style according to the older generations of the newer generation is that we have an increased tendency to indulge into small talk, according to their views, the newer generations have become shameless, we have lost all our traditions and cultural values, we don't value relations any more, for us the only thing that is important is money, monetary gains, gifts, shopping, following fashion trends, copying film stars, wasting our lives over social network, engage in temporary dating relations. According to older generations, youngsters have lost the essence of meaningful relations, our choices for engaging in sexual acts is destroying our cultures, the youngsters characters are judged on the basis of their sexual orientation, if an individual goes to their parents and opens up about being intimate with the person of the same sex, then for the parents, they have lost face in the society, for them, all the other acts are not sins, they will accept us if we rape someone, or steal something, kill somebody, molest someone, but if at all we tell them we want to marry our girlfriends, our boyfriends, then there is nothing worse than this.

It is as if, our sexual orientation of being gay has become a criteria to judge our sanity, we have some psychiatric illness for which treatment needs to be sought, or as if we are conversing in a language which isn't acceptable to them, they will judge us, try to hide us from meeting our neighbors, they will consult ojhaas to get us rid from the black magic or some witch craft which according to them must have influenced us. Sadly our sexual orientation becomes our identity, the probability of getting jobs, people attending our weddings etc also is based on our sexual identity. It is essential we become accepting of homosexuals and gays, because even they are normal human beings, and have feelings, their sexual preference doesn't make them the next wonder of the world, and their anatomy hasn't changed if they decide to marry or settle with their gay partners. And very sadly according to the individuals of our society who hold conventional views, this independent preference is destroying the rich heritage, not the forced sex by rapists, or domestic violence by husbands or remarks on a woman's character in news; all these disgusting things are acceptable and in fact they are remarks which are restoring our lost cultural heritage.

I really want to know does our generations zeal towards becoming self sufficient, independent, making their own decisions, fighting for their rights, wrong, are they against our cultural heritage, are they bringing shame to our country? And if the answer is yes and will not be accepted by conventional thinkers than justify the remarks that are made in public regarding woman's dresses, or blaming them for being victims to assaults, or stopping them to enter temples on religious grounds. Aren't all these things bringing shame to us, aren't these things pulling us back from becoming one of the developed countries, where at one end we are fighting to become technologically advanced and economically powerful and the other end our citizens aren't allowed to choose their sexual orientation on their own, girls aren't given the freedom to choose the clothing that they want to wear.

It is for all those who are looking for faults inside the youngsters, to look into their actions first and answer weren't in your times, birth of a female child considered inauspicious, wasn't the menstruating women secluded in a different room? Then why do we play the blame game. It is time we appreciate the efforts made by the youngsters in making our country proud by achieving medals for our country, by working with full passion and dynamism and holding the caliber to excel in everything that they set their foot in, it is time we stop focusing on irrelevant distracting things and in fact encourage them to achieve their endeavors, to become happy and satisfied, teach them well so that they stay away from hatred, violence, crime and corruption, and lastly to bring pride to our country by fighting the wrong together and raising their voices against the unjust.

Our country is not just facing problems from terrorism or black money, there are other prime important issues which need to be dealt courageously the issues of poverty, corruption, safety of youngsters from getting exploited under the influence of drugs, alcohol and lastly to protect our girls, who are being ridiculed in every segment, who are being used just because they are girls, hounds are looking to eat them up as if they are pieces of flesh dripping blood, India it is time, we stand united, it is time, we fight back.

9. Collectivistic Culture

Close your windows, draw your courtins, don't worry it's not a ghost that might come in but just your neighbor might have a peek inside your house or your lives; Yes the neighbor the same person who has no better business but to look for loop holes in our lives, but sorry to put it up this ways. It isn't just this poor neighbor who is problematic it's the whole society. Our culture is that of collectivism, where the values and needs of the others are valued more than our own personal needs, in our country, family and community are extremely important things, any decision we make is based on keeping the welfare of our families in our minds, any choices that we avail are well discussed primarily with our family members, etc. when we were kids we were taught the benefits of the same by our teachers and we felt really good, that we will always have our society to support us, our extended families will always be there to look after us, in some instances we always felt very proud of it, we felt stronger than others, because we stood united and we could fight any hardship. Without any doubt it did have many advantages for our mental and emotional health.

But nowadays it has lost its sole purpose of lifting one up when one felt down in the dumps. These days it's this collectivism which has become the root cause of evil. Where for providing everything instead of positivism and feeling happy about our achievements, this collectivistic culture has an opinion about our lifestyles and habits and very sadly the opinion isn't positive but just filled with criticism. If we are unmarried and aged around 30 then they will push our parents to look for suitable mate for us. Or if we are married then they will be worried about our unborn child and what will he grow up to be or sometimes when all is going well with our in laws, then they will ponder, how are we able to adjust with our in laws so well, if we have crossed the so called "appropriate age" of getting settled, then they will shower us with questions regarding the delays in following the stereotypical pattern of studying till 25 years of age, getting a job after it and then getting married by the time we turn 30, If we youngsters aren't following this monotonous routine, then according to our judgmental society, we are bringing bad name to our families, and then we are blamed by the conventional thinkers of our society regarding spoiling the Indian culture.

Now it's a real question from all those people who are proud of our collectivistic culture and the whole idea behind it, why do you close your eyes, when a father is asked to pay a huge amount of dowry to get his daughter married? Why do you close your ears and refrain yourself from hearing the screams of your daughter when she is getting molested by a bunch of monsters? Why do you become homophobic, when your daughters or sons want to get settled with their girlfriends and boyfriends respectively? Why do you make it a big deal and feel ashamed, if your child is diagnosed with a psychiatric disorder or contracts some sexually transmitted disease?

When the society faces issues such as these, where they genuinely need support from their neighbors, or the society, or their extended family members, then instead to standing true to our cultural values, we shower them with unwanted opinions, we humiliate them further, we blame them as much as we can; so that they are left with no other option, but to either turn into criminals for not having found justice in the first place, when they deserved it; or end their lives, because at any cost it is better than going through all the dishonor that they will face from the society.

www.ingramcontent.com/pod-product-compliance
Lightning Source LLC
Chambersburg PA
CBHW050756240726

48654CB00008B/517